G000108814

Research tool-kit

the how-to guide from *practical research for education*

volume 1
Edited by Alison Lawson

**National Foundation for
Educational Research**

How to cite a chapter in this publication
Hammond, P. (2008). 'An introduction to sampling.' In: Lawson, A.
(Ed). *Research Tool-kit: the How-to Guide from Practical Research for
Education* (Volume 1). Slough: NFER.

How to cite this publication
Lawson, A. (Ed). *Research Tool-kit: the How-to Guide from Practical
Research for Education* (Volume 1). Slough: NFER.

Design by Helen Crawley
Layout by Patricia Lewis

Published in July 2008 by the
National Foundation for Educational Research
The Mere, Upton Park
Slough, Berkshire SL1 2DQ

Contents

Foreword

Andrew Pollard, Director of the Teaching and Learning Research Programme

Teaching is a profession – but on what is that claim to professionalism based? The answer must basically lie in the forms of expertise that are developed as skill, knowledge, understanding and value commitment accumulate through experience. In the modern world though, we can't just claim this – we have to demonstrate it. And given the rapidity of change and the complexity of contemporary societies, we also have to update and renew this expertise constantly.

Practical research and enquiry, focused on the improvement of practice, makes an essential contribution to this process. It underpins reflective self-development and provides a continuous form of professional development. A particular strength is that it is under the control of the practitioner, and is thus often both empowering and fulfilling. Even more wonderfully, it is a way of improving the quality of what we are able to offer children, young people and other learners.

To engage in professional enquiry and research calls for knowledge – a skill expertise itself – which is where this Tool-kit comes in. In concise form, you have everything you need to get going. NFER is to be congratulated on its production. It should find its way to every staff room

July 2008

Introduction

Alison Lawson, Editor of *practical research for education*

I can't help but be fascinated by research. I've always been inquisitive, and have a questioning mind. As an undergraduate, my 'research' really went no further than reviewing literature and conducting a few interviews. Although I was interested, there was no rigour to what I was doing, and all my conclusions were based on data that was probably not all that good to begin with. Later, studying for a Masters in Business Administration, I was taught research methods, and that's when the bug really bit me. My MBA research project was exciting, and I soon signed up for a PhD. I was working as a lecturer at the time, and enjoyed teaching research methods and coaching students through their dissertations. In time, my career led me to the National Foundation for Educational Research, and to the job of Editor of their journal, *practical research for education*. I was – and still am – keen to instil that same excitement about research in others. But to be excited about it, you need to know how to do it.

The idea for a series of articles to help teachers and other education practitioners to do their own research came out of a discussion at an editorial panel meeting for the journal. It was 2004, and the journal was called *Topic* then – we re-launched in 2006 with the new name, *practical research for education*, to give readers a better idea of what the journal was all about. And it was precisely because the journal is all about research, and the practical implications of research, that it was important to try to equip people to do their own research projects, whether large or small. We wanted the series to give people the confidence to engage in research, giving them the knowledge and skills – the tools – to get started.

This book brings together the first six articles in the series. To begin, Mark Rickinson considers how to plan a research project. The planning is crucial – some extra thought at this stage saves a lot of work later on. Paula Hammond then examines the issue of sampling, explaining what is meant by 'sampling' and how one goes about drawing a sample from the total group available. Each kind of sample has its own advantages and disadvantages, and an explanation in plain English is invaluable. Before starting to gather information using a questionnaire or an interview, how do you know if you're asking the right questions? Caroline Sharp discusses this in the third instalment, in which she explains that asking questions is a special skill. She details when questions are used, what the main types of questions are, how they should be sequenced for best effect and which questions should be avoided.

One potentially daunting aspect of doing research is trying to find out what research has already been done in the area – finding the work that is already available, usually in the form of books and journal articles, can take a long time and result in masses of information. The next two chapters, by Alison Lawson and Pauline Benefield, deal with how to search for literature and what to do with the results of your search when you have them.

Research evidence from previously published sources, and from your own questionnaires or interviews, will give you a lot to go on, but there are other ways to gather more evidence. The last chapter discusses how to gather evidence from students – this is particularly useful in education settings, and it can be difficult to pull this sort of information together. Helen Betts and Bethan Burge draw on their own experience to outline some of the issues to consider when planning to collect this sort of information, and explain how real-life evidence from pupils can add richness, depth and a new perspective to a research project.

The Tool-kit series of articles from the journal *practical research for education* has proved to be popular not only with those involved in educational research, but for those working in social sciences more generally. In particular, the short format with illustrative examples is particularly good for students. For those who could not face ploughing through a long text book filled with academic jargon, the Tool-kit is ideal.

I hope that this collection will encourage you to embark on your own research project. And don't forget to share the results of your research with others – why not write it up and submit an article to *practical research for education*?

I look forward to hearing from you!

July 2008

1 Planning your research project

Often people realise too late that more time spent at the planning stage would have been a good idea. Thinking time before you embark on a project can be crucial to its eventual success. In this chapter, **Mark Rickinson** asks what research is, what it involves and how you can plan research so that it is effective.

What is this chapter about?

This chapter is about the process of planning research so that it is effective and manageable. It aims to provide:

- an overview of the research process
- guidance on planning a research project effectively
- case-study examples and ideas for effective planning
- links to other sources of information.

An overview of the research process

What is research?

A commonly cited definition of research is Lawrence Stenhouse's (1975) view of research as 'systematic inquiry made public'. This definition emphasises the systematic and enquiring nature of the activity, and the importance of sharing findings publicly. In schools and colleges, research can take many forms, ranging from individual projects to whole-school or network-wide initiatives (see Box 1.1).

What does research involve?

While the examples in Box 1.1 vary in many ways, it is possible to think of all of them going through a number of similar phases.

As shown in Figure 1.1, the research process can be seen as involving a number of interconnected phases. This first chapter in the Toolkit is concerned with how the initial planning phase can be carried out successfully.

Box 1.1 Examples of research

- Primary school reception staff undertaking classroom research on 'learning to learn' with support from senior staff and an external researcher.
- Two members of staff in an Early Years' Centre evaluating the use of video conferencing with young children, as part of the local Education Action Zone.
- A secondary school deputy headteacher doing a small research project to identify the curriculum needs of students at key stage 3 before investing in new materials.
- Several further education college tutors looking into the learning support needs of part-time learners as part of a regional Learning and Skills Research Network project.
- An individual teacher undertaking a project on staff development for a university research degree.

The planning phase

There are many things that need to be considered at the planning phase. One way of thinking about this is in terms of:

- getting the focus right

- getting the set-up right
- thinking about communication and impact.

Getting the focus right

This is about clarifying the research focus and questions (what?) and the research purposes (why?).

Research focus and questions

The first issue is identifying a topic to investigate, and the second is deciding on the questions to explore. Coming up with an interesting issue is often easier than working this into a clear, researchable question.

Ideas for research tend to emerge from people's interests and experiences. Topics can be stimulated by many different influences, such as a new development or initiative, a recurring difficulty, a conversation at a conference, a long-standing personal interest and/or another piece of research. It is important to remember that research requires time, motivation and commitment and so those carrying out the work need to be interested in the issue under investigation.

Moving from a research topic to a research question (or series of questions) is an important next step. This requires clear thinking on a number of levels. This is because good research questions need to be:

- clear – in terms of being as precise as possible in their wording. For example, the question 'What difficulties do year 3 pupils who do

Figure 1.1 The research process
Source: Morris and Norman (2004, p. 3)

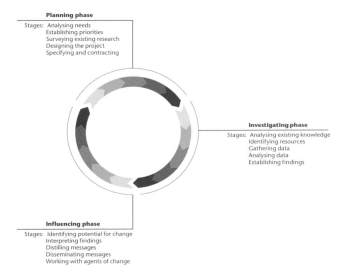

Planning phase

Stages: Analysing needs
Establishing priorities
Surveying existing research
Designing the project
Specifying and contracting

Investigating phase

Stages: Analysing existing knowledge
Identifying resources
Gathering data
Analysing data
Establishing findings

Influencing phase

Stages: Identifying potential for change
Interpreting findings
Distilling messages
Disseminating messages
Working with agents of change

not have computers at home experience during literacy lessons involving the use of a computer?', clearly specifies the focus (difficulties experienced), the age/type of pupils (year 3 pupils who do not have a computer at home) and the context (literacy lessons involving the use of a computer).

• practical – in terms of being questions that are possible to investigate and to answer. For example, an investigation into the effectiveness of a new type of curriculum provision would have more chance of answering a question such as 'What aspects of the provision do students like and dislike and why?', rather than one such as 'What impact does the provision have on students' long-term career progression?'.

• useful – in terms of focusing on aspects of an issue that are seen as important and potentially relevant/useful by other practitioners.

The formulation of good research questions can also be helped by thinking about the type of questions that need to be asked (see Box 1.2). Explanatory and exploratory questions tend to be more interesting but also more complex to research, compared with descriptive questions. However, descriptive questions should not be overlooked, as they are often an extremely important part of the picture and can help to inform the 'how and why' questions.

Box 1.2 Types of research question

Descriptive questions (What? Which? Where?)
e.g. Which ICT-based resources are most frequently used in this school?
Exploratory questions (How?)
e.g. How could we help students to feel safer in this school?
Explanatory questions (Why?)
e.g. Why have our attainment levels decreased over the last three years?

Box 1.3 Different purposes for research

- To evaluate impacts, i.e. to know what has/has not been achieved.
- To improve future practice, i.e. to identify areas for future improvement.
- To develop professionally, i.e. to develop new skills and insights.
- To ensure accountability, i.e. to demonstrate achievements to external bodies.
- To enable marketing, i.e. to publicise achievements internally or externally.

Research purposes

Being clear about the rationale for doing a piece of research is critical. Having well-articulated purposes can help with securing funding or other kinds of external support, encouraging people to take part in the study, keeping the researcher(s) motivated and focused, and identifying who the most important audiences are for the study's findings.

There can be a number of different motivations for carrying out research (see Box 1.3). An interesting way of thinking about the value of research is in terms of trying to reduce ignorance of some kind (Wagner, 1993). In thinking about research purposes, then, it might be helpful to ask: What or whose ignorance will this research help to reduce?

Getting the set-up right

Once the questions and purposes are clear, attention can turn to the practicalities of how the research is going to be done, by and with whom and over what time-scale.

Research methods

A crucial principle in planning research is that the research methods are driven by the research topic/questions (not the other way round). In other words, a research question like 'How do students feel about lessons in this department?' is likely to need some kind of interviewing of students, whereas 'Which ICT-based resources are most frequently used in this school?' might be answered with a questionnaire to staff. It is about selecting 'horses for courses', where the horses are the methods and the courses are the questions. Another way of describing this is in terms of selecting methods that are 'fit for purpose'. This can be helped by using a 'questions-methods' matrix, where one or more methods are selected for each of the research questions (see Figure 1.2).

No one research method is perfect and it is crucial to be aware of the strengths and weaknesses of different methods (see Box 1.4). It is also worth bearing in mind that the potential of different data-collection methods can be enhanced by using them in combination. Examples include:

- using interviews to generate ideas for survey questions

- following up on a survey with interviews to explore individuals' responses in more detail

- using observations of lessons as the starting point for student group discussions

- using a brief questionnaire at the start of a group discussion to get some quantifiable responses.

Research team and participants

There are two quite separate issues to think about here.

- Who will carry out the research?

- Who will take part in the research?

The first question is about deciding on the research team. An important consideration here is the skills that will be needed. A recent report about Collaborative Research in Practice (Morris and Norman, 2004) highlights three types of skills involved in research:

- methodological skills – being able to understand the strengths and weaknesses of different methods, as well as options for analysis and quality assurance

- managerial skills – relating to the coordination, scheduling and staffing of the project

Figure 1.2 A questions–methods matrix *Source: Adapted from Wellington (2000, p. 50)*

	Research methods					
Research questions	Questionnaire	Interview	Observation	Document analysis	etc.	etc.

Box 1.4 Strengths and weaknesses of different methods

Interviews, group discussions and conversations are useful for accessing:
- authentic voices and language
- verbal as opposed to written information
- depth of insights (perceptions, reasons, experiences)
- sensitive information
- information through dialogue
- unexpected information

but:
- they're costly/time consuming to undertake, write up and analyse
- audio/video recording can be inhibiting
- the data is not simple to analyse, and not easily quantifiable
- it's a skilled activity
- what people say is not always what they do.

Questionnaires, proformas and checklists are useful for accessing:
- large numbers of people's views
- anonymous views
- specific information
- comparative data
- information about many performance indicators at once
- quantifiable data

but:
- they're costly/time consuming to design, process and analyse
- questions can be misinterpreted or left blank
- response rates can be low
- responses may be superficial
- questions may not elicit the reasons behind a response.

Observation (structured or unstructured) is useful for accessing:
- insights into actions, interactions and processes
- non-verbal behaviours
- images or events to explore with participants
- rich descriptions or images

but:
- can inhibit those who are observed
- can alter the dynamics of what is being observed
- is costly/time-consuming to undertake and analyse
- can be difficult to analyse.

Journals and essays are useful for accessing:
- researchers' and participants' views and experiences during the process
- personal self-evaluative and reflective insights

but:
- can be demanding for researchers and participants
- can vary in the depth of insight provided.

Source: Adapted from Morris and Twitchin (1990, pp. 15–20)

- interpersonal skills – the capacity to engage different types of people and communicate effectively with potential user groups.

It is rare that all these skills will be found in one person, and that is why it is worth thinking about which other colleagues (internally and externally) might be encouraged to play a role (see Box 1.5). The use of a project advisory group comprising external individuals with particular skills is a useful way to complement the research team and promote wider awareness of the work.

Another issue relating to the question of 'Who will carry out the research?' is the possible tensions that can occur between being a practitioner and being a researcher. Such tensions can take the shape of practical concerns (such as 'Are students really going to tell me what they think about the lessons or should the interviews be done by someone else?') as well as deeper-seated identity issues ('How come people stop talking when I go into the team room now I am doing this research?').

The second question – Who will take part in the research? – is about sampling. In other words, from whom are we going to collect the information we need to answer our research questions? And, because it is almost always impossible to collect information from everyone in a particular group, how are we going to select a smaller number, i.e. a sample? A detailed discussion of sampling procedures is beyond the scope of this chapter, but it can be helpful to remember that:

- it is crucial to keep coming back to the research aims/questions in thinking about sampling
- where possible, it is usually beneficial to seek as much variety within your sample as possible
- the demands for variety need to be balanced with what is feasible and affordable (for the researchers and the participants).

Box 1.5 Sources of expertise for a research project

- An administrator with well-developed database or desktop publishing skills.
- An external researcher with knowledge of particular techniques or research literature.
- An information specialist who can help with internet searches.
- A senior manager who can help with dissemination across and beyond the school.
- A continuing professional development coordinator who can facilitate staff development sessions based on the research findings.
- A colleague from another school or college with a well-developed research culture.

Research schedule

Like other developments within schools and colleges, research needs careful scheduling. In developing research schedules, it is important to:

- ensure there is an opportunity to collect baseline (or starting point) data if this is needed

- build in time for piloting data-collection instruments such as focus group activities or questionnaires

- think carefully about what tasks need to take place before or after each other, e.g. sampling before data collection

- create opportunities for digesting and making sense of emerging ideas during the data-collection phase

- include dedicated time for analysis and discussion within the team

- allow time for formulating recommendations or 'take-away points' for other practitioner and policy audiences

- build in time for dissemination activities, both during as well as towards the end of the project.

Thinking about communication and impact

This final section concerns the big 'So what?' question. The key point is that if you wait until the end of your research project to think about dissemination, then you will have missed the boat! Questions of dissemination, communication and impact need to be thought about from the very start of a project and built into schedules and budgets.

A central challenge is thinking as creatively as possible about how research findings and research products can be communicated and made meaningful to their intended audiences. This requires careful consideration about who the intended audiences are and what their preferences might be in terms of mode and style of communication (see Table 1.1).

In planning a dissemination strategy, though, it is important to remember that this needs to be as active as possible. In other words, the challenge is not to scatter your

possible tensions can occur between being a practitioner and being a researcher

Table 1.1   Different methods of dissemination

Mode of communication	Possible methods
Paper	Project summary leaflets
	Key findings leaflets
	Project newsletters/bulletins
	Posters, postcards and displays
	Articles in professional journals
	Teaching or teacher-training materials
	Practitioner toolkits
	Articles in academic journals
	Books
Electronic	Project websites
	Online project summaries
	Online key findings summaries
	Project newsletters/bulletins
	Project videos/CD ROMs/DVDs
	Targeted email distribution lists
	Practitioner-research websites, e.g. *Topic online*
Events	Advisory group meetings
	Project seminars
	Informal discussions with key partners/networks
	Training events/workshops
	Implications workshops
	Policy discussion forums
	Presentations at practitioner conferences
	Presentations at academic conferences
Media	Press releases
	TV/radio interviews
	Newspaper articles

research findings as far as possible, but rather to help others to engage with your work and see how it might be useful in their contexts. This can be helped by:

- tailoring dissemination methods to audience interests and needs
- using approaches that enable two-way, face-to-face communication
- using a range of different methods in combination
- involving target users in planning dissemination methods/events

- recruiting well-known opinion leaders/experts as project 'champions' (for more details, see Nutley *et al.*, 2003).

A final word

As a final word about planning research, please remember that:

- it is usually better to start small with simple questions/data-collection methods, rather than getting bogged down in collecting masses of data that will never be analysed or used

- the research process is cyclical and haphazard (as opposed to linear and tidy) and so plans need to be flexible and responsive – indeed, it is often when things 'go wrong', that the most interesting findings are becoming clear!

Further information

Bell, A.J. (1993). *Doing Your Research Project*. Buckingham: Open University Press.

Gillham, B. (2000). *Developing a Questionnaire*. London: Continuum.

Gillham, B. (2000). *The Research Interview*. London: Continuum.

Handscomb, G. and MacBeath, J. (2003). *The Research Engaged School*. Essex: Forum for Learning and Research Enquiry (FLARE), Essex County Council.

Morris, A. (2004). *From Idea to Impact: a Guide to the Research Process*. London: Learning and Skills Research Centre.

MacBeath, J., Demetriou, H., Rudduck, J. and Myers, K. (2003). *Consulting Pupils: a Toolkit for Teachers*. Cambridge: Pearson.

Robson, C. (2002). *Real World Research: a Resource for Social Scientists and Practitioner–Researchers*. Oxford: Blackwell.

References

Morris, A. and Norman, L. (2004). *Collaborative Research in Practice*. London: Learning and Skills Research Centre.

Morris, M. and Twitchin, R. (1990). *Evaluating Flexible Learning: a Users' Guide*. Slough: NFER.

Nutley, S., Solesbury, W. and Percy-Smith, J. (2003). *Models of Research Impact: A Cross-sectoral Review of Literature and Research*. London: Learning and Skills Research Centre.

Stenhouse, L. (1975). *An Introduction to Curriculum Research and Development*. London: Heinemann.

Wagner, J. (1993). Ignorance in educational research: or how can you 'not' know that?, *Educational Researcher*, 22, 5, 15–23.

Wellington, J. (2000). *Educational Research. Contemporary Issues and Practical Approaches*. London: Continuum

Related weblinks

www.topiconline.co.uk/index_1.asp
The NFER's online summaries of research for schools and teachers.
www.gtce.org.uk/research/romhome.asp
The General Teaching Council's research page for practitioners, entitled 'Research of the Month'.
www.standards.dfes.gov.uk/research
The Department for Education and Skills' Research Informed Practice site with searchable digests of research.

www.nerf-uk.org/bulletin/
The National Educational Research Forum's research bulletin for teachers in schools and colleges.
www.lsda.org.uk/files/lsda/solutions/OrganisationalDev/RDToolkit.pdf
The Learning and Skills Development Agency's Research and Development Toolkit.
www.tta.gov.uk/itt/providers/research/panel/index.htm
The website of the National Teacher Research Panel, an advisory body of teacher researchers.
www.teachernet.gov.uk/research/
The Department for Education and Skills' information service for education professionals interested in all aspects of research.
www.becta.org.uk/research/display.cfm?section=6
The Becta website includes a section on practitioner research, including advice about how to go about doing research and about ethics.

About the author

Mark Rickinson is an educational research consultant specialising in programme evaluation, outdoor/environmental education, research training and literature reviews. He is currently undertaking work for the Department for Education and Skills, the National Educational Research Forum, the Countryside Agency and Learning through Landscapes. Mark is also a Research Fellow at Oxford University Department of Educational Studies.

Address for correspondence

Dr Mark Rickinson
Educational Research Consultant
19 Egerton Road, wallingford,
Oxfordshire, OX10 0HL
01494 839586
m.rickinson@dsl.pipex.com

2 An introduction to sampling

What is sampling, how does one draw a sample from the total group available, and what are the advantages and disadvantages of different kinds of sample? **Paula Hammond** explains how to use a sample in your research.

What is this chapter about?

This chapter is about the process of drawing a sample to conduct a piece of research, and aims to provide:

- an overview of the sampling process
- guidance on drawing a sample
- links to other sources of information
- a glossary of technical terms.

An overview of the sampling process

What is sampling?

Since before the existence of the Domesday book, there has been an interest in measuring the properties of large collections of individuals or objects. Such a collection, in which we are interested, is known as a population (see Box 2.1).

Sometimes, like the 10-yearly census, we attempt to record every member of our population. This is not always practical or economically efficient, so a much more appropriate approach is to take a sample, or small portion of the population in which we are interested. From examining the properties of this sample we hope to be able to draw conclusions about the population. The fundamental question is how such a sample should be drawn to provide the best and most accurate information.

Box 2.1 Examples of populations

- All children in England and Wales whose 7th birthday is between 1 September 1998 and 31 August 1999
- All maintained secondary schools in England
- All pupils in maintained secondary schools in England

What sampling methods are there?

There are three methods of sampling:

1. convenience sampling – choose the most convenient or accessible members of the population

2. judgemental sampling – choose individuals who you believe represent the population

3. random sampling – choose sample members completely randomly.

If a school wishes to pick a sample of 25 pupils to represent the whole school population of 500, these three approaches might be implemented as follows:

1. grab the first 25 pupils who walk past the staff room

2. think of 25 pupils covering all ranges of ability

3. put all 500 names in a hat and pull out 25 at random.

What can be said about these methods?

Convenience sampling has nothing to recommend it, except that it is convenient. The first 25 pupils who walk past the staff room may be quite unrepresentative of the school population. The worst examples of convenience samples are 'self-selecting' samples, e.g. where people respond to questionnaires in the media. Only those people who are interested enough are likely to respond to the questionnaire.

Judgemental sampling seems to be a much better approach, but it all depends on the accuracy of the judgement. The results from this method of sampling are open to criticism from those who do not agree with your judgement. This whole method is open to all kinds of bias, and there is no way of knowing whether the sample is representative or not.

Random sampling seems to have a bit of a negative connotation attached to it, but all it actually means is that every individual in the population has an equal chance of appearing in the sample. Random sampling has two advantages over the other two approaches. Firstly, it is objective in the sense that no subjective judgement is involved. Secondly, it uses statistical theory to estimate the errors involved in taking the sample results to approximate the population characteristics. This is not possible using the other two approaches.

For these reasons random sampling is the preferred approach, and the temptation to use judgemental sampling should be avoided. It may seem ironic that 'random' selection is preferred to careful use of knowledge and judgement, but this is fundamental to choosing a truly representative sample.

Desirable properties of samples

There are two aspects of samples that relate to how well they estimate the underlying characteristics of the population from which they are drawn. Both can be thought of as the 'average' properties of the samples, assuming that different samples are drawn from the same population, and then their results are compared with each other and the population.

Bias is a measure of the extent to which the samples accurately estimate the population properties, on average. Ideally, bias should be zero. Some samples may overestimate and others may underestimate, but on average they should get it correct. If the bias is very different from zero, then there is a serious problem with the sampling.

Precision is a measure of the extent to which the results of different samples agree. One of the determining factors here is the size of the sample; very roughly, the precision is related to the square root of the sample size. If there is a need to double the precision then a sample four times as big would be required.

Figure 2.1 illustrates these ideas in terms of the spread of bullets (dots) hitting a target (circles). In archery or shooting the idea is to get the arrows or bullets as close to the centre as possible. This is also true for drawing a sample – we want to get the sample estimates (bullets) as close as possible

to the population value (target centre). In the top left-hand corner we have high bias and low precision; not only are the sample estimates likely to be a long way from each other, they are not even right 'on average'. This would correspond to a very small sample (low precision) with an unrepresentative sampling methodology – for example, trying to estimate the national proportion of Conservative voters using a small sample of Surrey stockbrokers!

The bottom left-hand corner shows high bias coupled with higher precision – there is not much uncertainty in the sample estimate, but it is definitely wrong. Perhaps a very large sample of Surrey stockbrokers?

In the top right-hand corner is the opposite situation – low bias but also low precision. Here we might have drawn a nationally representative sample of the electorate, but made it rather small. Although we are right 'on average', the result from our sample has a fair amount of uncertainty.

Ideally, when drawing a sample it is best to aim for low bias and high precision, as in the bottom right-hand picture. If this cannot be achieved, however, it is better to ensure that the sample is unbiased. Low precision can be dealt with by increasing the sample size. If a sample is biased, however, this is a fundamental problem that needs to be dealt with by a review of the way in which the sample was drawn.

Figure 2.1 Illustration of bias and precision in sampling

High bias, low precision

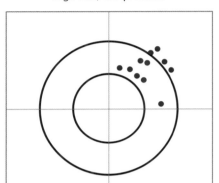

Low bias, low precision

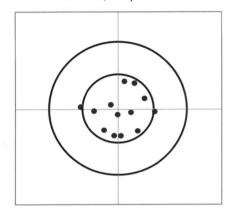

High bias, high precision

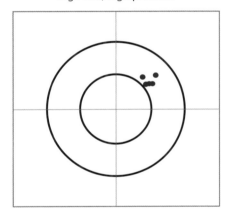

Low bias, high precision

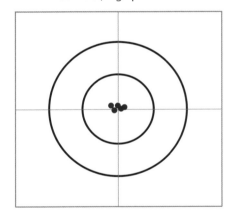

Sampling frames

The sampling frame is a list or database that contains all the members of the desired population from which the sample is to be drawn (see Box 2.2). It is an essential prerequisite for successful sampling – if the sampling frame is incomplete or flawed, then the sample maybe unrepresentative of the population. The wrong choice of sampling frame can lead to big errors. Sampling frames do not have to be 100 per cent accurate to be useful. No database is ever perfect, and a few random errors are unlikely to have a significant effect on the quality of the sample.

Box 2.2 Examples of sampling frames

Population	Sampling frame
All adults in a borough	Electoral roll
Children in a class	Class register
Staff in a school	Personnel staff list
Schools in England and Wales	Database of school information

Sampling methods

Simple random sampling

This is the simplest form of sampling methodology. Essentially, each member of the population is assigned the same probability of being in the sample, and a specified number of individuals are randomly drawn. For a visual representation, think of a big hat into which all the names of the population are placed and then a name is pulled out one at a time – this is also known as sampling without replacement. As each member of the population has the same probability of being drawn, the

sample is unbiased. The precision can be calculated easily, and is proportional to the square root of the number in the sample.

There are a few disadvantages to this method – the first being inconvenience, as it is not always possible to put all the names of the members of the population into a big hat, and secondly there can be problems with sub-populations. An actual sample may leave out, or be unrepresentative of, important sections in the population, e.g. it may not include members of a particular ethnic group.

Stratified random sampling

This is a variation of simple random sampling, and takes into account the fact that the population may be divided into distinct sub-populations (strata). Taking into consideration the strata makes the sample more representative and improves the precision. The method is similar to simple random sampling, except that a separate sample is drawn within each stratum and then these are combined to give the overall sample. To improve the efficiency of the sample it is best to select strata that are potentially linked to the outcome of the survey (see Box 2.3).

Quota sampling

This method of sampling is commonly used be market research organisations, and is superficially similar to stratified random sampling. The population is divided into 'quotas', similar to the

Box 2.3 Example of stratified sampling

If a sample of 50 pupils is required from a large secondary school that has five equal year groups (years 7 to 11), it would be sensible to define the strata as equal to the year groups and randomly select 10 pupils from each year group to get a sample of the whole school.

Box 2.4 Example of quota sampling

An interview is conducted with a sample of boys and girls across a range of ages. Using the school roll, the researcher calculates the proportion of pupils in each of the 'quotas' (see Table 2.1).

Table 2.1 Quota sampling

Gender	Age (years)					
	5	6	7	8	9	10
% Boys	12	16	15	20	22	15
% Girls	16	20	16	21	15	12

Using Table 2.1, 20 per cent of the boys and 21 per cent of the girls in the sample should be eight years old.

strata mentioned above, and a specified number of individuals are chosen to make up each quota. The main difference is that within each quota the sample members are not drawn randomly, but by using a combination of opportunity and judgement. As random sampling is not used, the bias and precision of this approach cannot be estimated. Quota sampling is not really ideal for school surveys because of mobile and changing populations (see Box 2.4).

Cluster sampling

If the members of the population are grouped together into larger units, and access to the population is necessary via these units, then it may be necessary, or administratively desirable, to sample first the units and then the population members within the sampled units. This is known as cluster sampling, and is what happens when schools are sampled and then pupils

within those schools are sampled. Alternatively, you might sample classes in the school and then pupils in those classes (see Box 2.5).

Option 1 is the simplest method for administrative purposes and requires no sampling within schools, but it would probably not provide a representative picture of schools across the country. Option 3 would be statistically attractive but administratively difficult. Option 2 provides a fair balance between conflicting demands; there are plenty of classes to give a good chance of a representative sample but administratively taking ten pupils per class is not too difficult.

Design effects

When simple random sampling is not used, the precision of the sample for a given sample size changes. Stratified sampling can improve precision; cluster sampling can make it worse. One way of quantifying the extent to which the precision of a sample is better or worse than for simple random sampling is through using the 'design effect'.

The design effect is a number that shows how much larger or smaller a sample you need to have in order to get the same precision as a simple random sample. This is related to the extent to which individuals within the same cluster are similar to each other in what you're measuring. For example, if you were studying genetic factors, drawing extra individuals from the same family (who are likely to be similar to those you have already sampled) would give you less new information than drawing them from different families. Similar effects can happen in schools and classes – individuals in the same school or class may be more similar than those in different schools and classes.

Sample sizes

Here are a couple of simple examples to illustrate the kind of sample sizes you might need to estimate population

> ### Box 2.5 Example of cluster sampling
>
> If a sample of 200 pupils is required and there are 20 pupils of the required age in each class, then three options could be used:
>
> 1. draw 10 classes, and take all 20 pupils in each class
>
> 2. draw 20 classes, and then randomly select 10 pupils in each class
>
> 3. draw 50 classes, and then randomly select two pupils in each class.

values in different circumstances. Suppose you want to estimate the proportion of year 9 pupils achieving a certain level in a subject both nationally and within a given school, and in each case you want to do so with a 95 per cent confidence interval, which is plus or minus five percentage points. Assume also that we know the proportion is likely to be around 0.5 or 50 per cent.

Nationally, there are about 500,000 year 9 pupils. You draw a random sample of schools and one class of 25 in each school to get your estimate – this is a clustered sample. There is a simple formula that says that to get a 5 per cent precision with a simple random sample you would need 384 cases, i.e. 15 schools. However, because pupils in the same school and class are likely to be similar, there is a design effect that can be estimated as 5.8. We need to multiple the total required sample by this value to get 2228 pupils in 89 schools. This is equivalent to 0.4% of the whole population.

To get the same precision in a single school, say with 200 year 9 pupils, there is a more complicated formula that takes account of the fact that the sample is likely to be a sizeable fraction of the population. On the other hand, there is no design effect because we are only interested in the results for this school. The required sample size using the formula is 99 pupils, almost 50 per cent of the population. So to get the same precision as the national sample we need fewer pupils in total but a much bigger proportion of the population.

Final word

The following summarises the main steps involved in using a sample to conduct research.

1. Determine the research issues that the sample will address, and ensure that the sample will be the most effective way of investigating these.

2. Decide on the population from which the sample will be drawn, and the sampling frame that will be used to draw the sample.

3. Decide on the size of the achieved sample required, either by considering the required precision for key estimates or using other criteria.

4. Estimate the expected response rate.

5. Determine the key variables by which the sample will be stratified.

6. Draw the sample from the sampling frame.

grab the first 25 pupils who walk past the staff room

Glossary of terms

Bias
In general, this refers to any situation in which there is an unwanted influence acting on the data collected, in such a way that it no longer properly represents the desired population. Any conclusions we draw from a biased sample are not necessarily valid for the wider population.

Cluster sampling
Cluster sampling operates when members of the population are grouped together into larger units (sometimes called 'primary sampling units' or PSUs), and access to the population is necessarily via these units (e.g. pupils within schools). This may lead to reduced precision and increased design effect.

Design effect
The design effect (deff) is a number that shows how much larger or smaller a sample you need to get the same precision as a simple random sample.

Mean
The conventional way of calculating the 'average' of a set of data values, by adding them up and dividing by the number of data values. Can be seriously affected by a few extreme data values.

Population
All the members of a group of interest, e.g. all schools in England and Wales or the employers of graduates in Berkshire.

Precision
A measure of the extent to which the statistics computed from a set of samples would be consistent and reproducible.

Quota sampling
An approach in which the population is divided into subsets and a required quota is set for the sample from each subset. To fill each quota, members are selected using judgement and opportunity sampling. The bias and precision of this approach cannot be estimated.

Sample
A subset of members of a population that represents that population and on which measurements are taken to reflect the properties of the whole population.

Sampling
The drawing of a fraction or sample of all the members of a population that is representative of that population.

Sampling fraction
The percentage of the population represented in the sample.

Sampling frame
A list or database containing details of all or most of the members of the desired population, from which a sample is to be drawn.

Simple random sampling
The simplest sampling procedure. All members of the population are drawn with equal probability, without replacing them in the population. Each member of the sample is drawn independently of the rest.

Standard deviation
A measure of the spread of some quantity within a group of individuals. If the quantity is distributed approximately Normally, we would expect about 95 per cent of the individuals to be within two standard deviations either side of the mean value.

Statistic
A statistic is any numerical value computed from a set of data, whose aim is to represent the data in some way and from whose value a statistical judgement may be made. A example is the mean or arithmetical average of a set of numbers, often used as a measure of its 'central tendency'.

Stratified random sampling
This variation of simple random sampling allows the population to be divided into subsets or 'strata'. Within each stratum the sample is drawn randomly, and these sub-samples are combined to give the overall sample. If the variance in the variable being measured is lower within strata, then this method can improve the precision of the sample and decrease the design effect.

Variable
A characteristic of members of the population, e.g. the number of pupils in the school or the score on a key stage 2 English test.

Further reading

Barnett, V. (1981). *Elements of Sampling Theory*. Sevenoaks: Hodder & Stoughton.
Fielding, J. and Gilbert, N. (2000). *Understanding Social Statistics*. London: Sage Publications.
Fink, A. (1995). *How to Sample in Surveys*. London: Sage Publications.
Kish, L. (1995). *Survey Sampling*. New York: Wiley.
Schagen, I. (2000). *Statistics for School Managers*. Suffolk: Courseware.
Schagen, I. (2004), Data – does it really speak for itself? Or why do a complicated analysis when you can get it wrong much more easily with a simple analysis? *Topic* 31.

Weblinks

www.edubase.gov.uk
DfES Edubase
www.statistics.gov.uk
National Office of Statistics
www.becta.org.uk
British Educational Communications and Technology Agency
www.rss.org.uk
Royal Statistical Society
www.statscom.gov.uk
Statistics Commission

About the author

Paula Hammond is a senior statistician at the NFER. Her recent work includes development of National Curriculum assessment, analysis of 'value-added' school performance data and the evaluation of large-scale educational initiatives, particularly the National Literacy and Numeracy Strategies, the analysis of the year 3, 4 and 5 optional tests and the evaluation of the university summer schools. She also has expertise in age standardisation methods and is especially interested in the impact of feedback to schools.

Contact details

Paula Hammond
paula.hammond@o2.com

3 Are you asking the right questions?

Asking questions in research is an art. When are questions used, what are the main types of questions, how should you sequence them and which questions should you avoid? **Caroline Sharp** outlines some of the things to think about when using questions in research.

What is this chapter about?

This chapter is about using questions in different ways throughout the research process. It aims to provide:

- an overview of the uses of questions in research

- different types of questions and how to use them

- questions to avoid or use with caution

- guidance on question wording and sequencing

- links to further sources of information.

Why focus on questions?

I know that many readers will be contemplating their School Evaluation Forms and wondering what evidence to provide. Gathering the views of pupils and parents can be particularly challenging, and a good quality self-evaluation depends on asking the right questions. This chapter aims to help you think about some of the issues involved in asking questions, whether for self-evaluation or a broader investigation.

asking questions is an art-form in itself

Table 3.1 Using questions at different stages of research

Stage of the research process	Asking questions
Planning phase	Establishing your research questions and making sure they are clear, practical and useful.
	Selecting your sample (which pupils, staff members, parents etc?).
	Asking 'What other information/research/expertise already exists to help us?'
Investigating phase	Devising your data collection strategy and designing your 'instruments' (e.g. questionnaires, interview questions).
	Checking whether your questions are suitable.
	Using questions to help in analysing your data.
Interpreting phase	Using questions to interpret your data. What does it mean? Why have we got these results? What are the key messages from this research?
Influencing phase	Reporting outcomes. What do we want to say to whom? What is the best method of sharing the results of this research? Who needs to do what in order to improve practice? How will this be achieved?

Doing research is a wonderful excuse for nosiness: it gives you permission to ask questions of complete strangers and their answers provide a fascinating insight into another world. But asking questions is an art-form in itself. There is nothing more frustrating than getting to the end of a research project and realising that you asked too many of the wrong questions and not enough of the right ones. It is for this reason that I thought it might be useful to focus on questioning as a fundamental part of the research process.

When do you use questions in research?

The most obvious use of questions in research is during data collection. But questions provide the key to every stage of the research process, from deciding what you are going to research, right through to sharing your results (see Table 3.1).

Figure 3.1 Using research questions to focus research

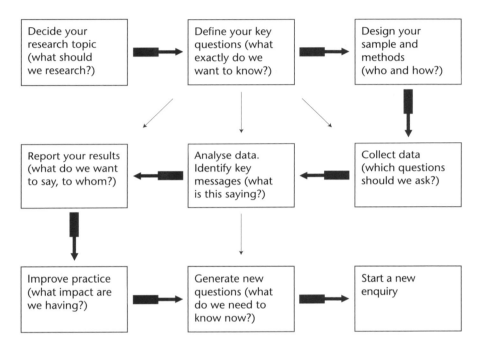

As Mark Rickinson pointed out in chapter 1, once you have decided what you want to research, the next step is to identify your key research questions. In many ways, your research questions form the backbone of the research, as you should return to them to help make decisions about your design, sample, data collection and analysis.

Figure 3.1 shows how research questions influence decisions taken at different stages of a research project.

For example, the questions you ask during data collection should be strongly influenced by the research questions, as should the process of analysis and reporting. Of course, new questions sometimes occur during the research process – especially during data collection and analysis. It is important to take account of these and make a decision about what to do – can you include them in your current analysis and reporting; can you investigate them in a new enquiry?

What are the main types of question?

Six main types of question form the basis for most of the others you might wish to ask. These are shown in Box 3.1.

When devising your research questions, such as questionnaires and interview schedules, it can be helpful to consider how you expect people to answer. For largely factual questions, a closed-ended question (i.e. one with a limited and predictable number of responses) may be suitable. This is particularly appropriate for simple factual questions, of the 'what, when, where, who' variety. Examples of closed-ended questions include:

- Do you have a teaching qualification? (Yes/No)

- When do you usually leave for school in the morning? (Between 6.00 and 8.15am)

- Do you usually sit next to a boy or a girl in class? (Boy/girl/no usual pattern).

Open-ended questions are more suitable for exploratory or explanatory questions, like 'why', 'how' or 'in what way'. These questions usually require some reflection from the respondent and are likely to generate a variety of answers. Examples of open-ended questions include:

- How do you adapt your teaching methods when working in a larger class?

Box 3.1 Six questions according to Kipling

Rudyard Kipling memorably identified six types of question in the following poem, which appeared in the 'Just So' stories:

I keep six honest serving men
They taught me all I knew:
Their names are What and Why
and When
And How and Where and Who.

Kipling, 1902

These questions can be used at different stages of research. They can help in initial planning and also to define questions for data collection. Here are some examples of the six types of questions applied to research.

Research planning stage	Data collection stage
What do we want to investigate?	What is your role?
Why do we want to know?	Why did you apply for this post?
When should we start do the research?	When did you work here?
How should we do it?	How do you do plan your work?
Where should we look for information?	Where do you hold sports events?
Who should be part of the research team?	Who receives this newsletter?

- Why do you think children performed less well in reading this year?
- What do you feel are the benefits of adopting this method?

Occasionally, questions that seem open-ended are actually quite 'closed':

- How would you rate the quality of this instruction manual?

Bear in mind that closed questions take less time to answer, whereas open questions are more time-consuming but are likely to result in a more satisfying experience for the respondent.

Considering whether you are asking a closed- or open-ended question is useful because it:

- ensures that you are clear about the kind of information you are seeking

- helps you to design an appropriate format for the question (and answer)

- can help you think about balance and sequencing.

Which questions should you avoid?

There are some kinds of questions that are best avoided or used only with caution. Be especially wary of asking any questions that are unduly complicated, leading or venture into sensitive territory.

Complicated questions

A question may be complicated because it is too long, contains too many parts or contains unfamiliar words. Complicated questions are likely to confuse respondents and make them feel ill at ease.

Solution: Revisit the question and decide what you really want to know. Avoid vague or complex ideas and cut down on the number of subordinate clauses. Make sure you are using simple, familiar language and consider breaking the question down into a series of shorter questions.

Original version of a complicated question

Please could you tell me when you started work what was your experience of the hierarchy of management structure in place and are you of the same opinion now with regards to this organisation following the reorganisation?'

Revised version

As you know, this organisation has recently been restructured. In your opinion, what difference has it made to the management structure? How has it affected your line management?

Leading questions

Leading questions suggest that the questioner expects a particular answer. This is likely to make your respondent feel under pressure to give the 'right' answer and risks biasing your results.

Solution: Check whether your question is (or could appear to be) leading and find an alternative approach.

Original example of a leading question

1. I take it that you agree with the school's policy on behaviour management?

Revised version

1. How do you usually deal with the following aspects of behaviour management?
a) Pupils who distract others in class
b) Pupils who are rude/abusive to you
c) Pupils who are accused of bullying by other pupils?
(You can later analyse the responses to this question in relation to the school's behaviour management policy.)
2. Do you feel that the school's policy could be improved? If yes, how? (What type of improvements would you like to see?)

Sensitive questions

Sensitive questions ask the respondent to reveal something that they may feel uncomfortable about discussing. This type of question should only be used if there is a strong argument for collecting the information. An obvious area of sensitivity concerns someone's personal background, such as their ethnicity or religion. Such questions may be seen as unduly intrusive and unnecessary. On the other hand, studies of issues affecting minority ethnic groups or people from different religious affiliations can provide valuable information for research, in which case it would be important to find out.

It is also worth thinking about the potential sensitivity of other, less obvious questions, such as those concerning someone's age, qualifications, years of experience or even whether people are familiar with a piece of legislation. A respondent may suspect that there is a hidden agenda behind the question: 'They want to know my age – do they think I'm too young/old for this job?' or 'They mentioned the latest legislation – they must expect me to know all about it.'

Another area of sensitivity may be raised by asking people to reveal something about themselves that they feel may not be socially acceptable. This could apply to aspects of their behaviour or views about a contentious issue.

Solution: Be aware which questions are sensitive and avoid them if possible. If you really need to know, make sure you are behaving ethically, explain why you want the information and find an appropriate way of requesting it (you could offer people the option of not responding, if they do not wish to answer more personal questions). Rather than asking open-ended questions in areas of sensitivity, it may be appropriate to predict a range of answers and offer these to respondents for them to indicate their agreement or disagreement (this approach has been adopted in health education for the finding out about aspects of people's sexual behaviour that may put them at risk). While the above examples may seem obvious, it is not always quite so easy to distinguish the clear from the confusing, the unbiased from the leading or the fair from the insensitive. This is why it is important to draft, redraft and try out questions before you use them. For further advice on this process, see below under 'Have you asked the right questions?'

How should you sequence your questions?

Once you have compiled a set of questions, you will need to decide the order in which to ask them. It helps the recipient to follow your line of thinking if you put questions into a logical order and group them according to broad themes. Simple, introductory questions placed at the

Original version of a sensitive question

What is your ethnic group?

Revised version

Previous research has shown that there is a low take-up of our services from certain ethnic groups. We are asking people if they would be willing to tell us their ethnic backgrounds so we can ensure our services appeal to everyone. This information is voluntary and will be handled in confidence. If you are willing to help us in this way, please tick the box which best represents your ethnic background:

Black, African ☐
Black, Caribbean ☐
Black, other ☐
Indian ☐
Pakistani ☐
Bangladeshi ☐
Mixed ethnicity ☐
Chinese ☐
White, European ☐
White, other ☐
Other ethnic group ☐
(please specify).................

beginning will help your respondents to relax and encourage them to carry on to the end. Slightly more personal (potentially sensitive) questions may be best placed at the end of the sequence.

Once you have divided your questions into content areas, you can consider how to sequence them within each section. You may decide to put shorter, more factual (largely closed-ended) questions at the beginning. This can help to ease the respondent into providing information and can help you to establish the basic facts before asking broader or more opinion-based questions. On the other hand, you could decide to start with a broader question and narrow down into a specific area of interest, guiding the respondent onto a particular path or line of questioning. It may help you to visualise this by thinking about it as using a funnel, pyramid or diamond/hour glass shape.

Funnelling can be a useful questioning process to get from the more general to the specific. It begins with open questions and builds upon them with increasing narrowness.

1. Could I start by asking you to outline your main areas of responsibility at work?

2. Are there any areas of your work where you would welcome some additional training?

3. What did you think of the management training you recently completed?

4. Which parts did you find the most useful?

5. Have you found any of it difficult to apply in practice? If yes, Which parts have you found most difficult to apply?

The pyramid sequence begins with a more specific (possibly closed-ended) question at the apex of the pyramid and moves to a more general level of enquiry (providing a broader base). This can be used to ease people into the process of answering your questions.

1. Are you a member of the tennis club?

2. How often do you manage to play?

3. Do you always play with the same partners? (Which ones?)

4. How could the club's facilities be improved to encourage more social tennis?

The **diamond sequence** is a combination of the two sequences described above. It begins with a restricted question, moving to more open ones and then narrows down to more specific questions. The **hour glass** is another combination, but in the reverse order, starting with a broader topic, narrowing down and then broadening out again towards the end.

Have you asked the right questions?

Once you have a draft set of questions, it is worth checking whether you have asked the right ones. This entails considering relevance, question wording and sequencing.

First, you need to work out whether you have addressed your key research questions (it is all too easy to 'drift' away from answering your research questions when drafting research questions). Sometimes you will discover that you have asked a similar question but have missed out on a vital piece of information, so make sure you have included everything you need.

It might be helpful to use a simple grid to check the degree of overlap between the research questions/areas of interest and the questions in the interview schedule or questionnaire

Table 3.2 gives an example showing the main research themes for different groups of interviewees. The researcher has drawn up the matrix and then gone through the interview schedules noting the question numbers that address each theme. Question numbers in brackets indicate questions that are not specifically focussed on the theme, but the answers may provide some relevant information. Using a matrix like this will soon show up any discrepancies in the coverage of your main areas of interest.

A common pitfall when drafting research questions is to ask too many questions, so try to cut out any that are not strictly necessary. A good test of this is to predict the kind of answers you are likely to get from each question and then see whether the information is really vital to your research (where will it fit into your report or presentation of results?). You will probably find you have included a few questions you thought might generate interesting information, but are not strictly relevant to your current focus. If you don't edit them out now you risk wasting a lot of time in

Table 3.2 Matrix of interview questions by research themes

	Relation to learning and teaching strategy	Development of teaching practices	Longer-term professional learning and progression	Value for money
Programme leaders	10, 11	7, 8	6, 9	12
Programme participants	9, 10	6, 7 (3, 4)	2, 8	11
HODs	7, 8	5 (2, 3)	6, (4)	9

collecting and analysing information you may never use.

Once you have refined your questions, the best way of identifying problems with wording or sequencing is to conduct a trial run or 'pilot'. Ideally, this involves testing out your draft questions on a group of people who are similar to the people in your sample (e.g. if you intend to ask questions of teachers in your own school, you could pilot the questions on teachers at a neighbouring school). You should aim to administer the questions in a similar way to that you have planned for the 'real' study. If you cannot manage a pilot, you could attempt a simulation, by asking friends and colleagues to assume the identity of your respondent group and help you test out your questions. Look out for any questions that cause people to hesitate, ask for clarification or lead to misinterpretation. These problems may be due to difficulties with wording (see 'questions to avoid') or sequencing – your respondents may not be able to follow your structure. It also gives you a chance to assess how long it will take to complete the interview/questionnaire.

When you have completed your pilot or trial, you should be able to spot problem areas and make amendments before you use the questions with your intended respondent group.

What next?

This chapter has outlined some points to consider when using questions in research. As mentioned above, the questioning doesn't stop when the data collection is complete. Questions are an invaluable tool for honing investigative skills. You can use them as a way of interrogating your data, deciding its implications (the 'so what?' question) and even in presenting the outcomes of your research. You could even try posing questions as subheadings in a report or presentation, as I have in this chapter – it's a good discipline to keep you focused on the topic in hand.

References

Kipling, R. (1902). *Just So Stories*. London: Walker Books Ltd.

Further reading

Bell, J. (1988). *Doing Your Research Project: A Guide for First-Time Researchers in Education, Health and Social Science*. Milton Keynes: OUP.

Robson, C. (2002). *Real World Research*, second edn. Oxford: Blackwell Publishers.

Patton, M.Q. (1997). *Utilization-focused Evaluation: the new century text*, third edn. London: Sage.

About the author

Caroline Sharp is a principal research officer at the NFER. Her main research interests are early years education (especially season of birth), leadership, study support and arts and creativity. She has a particular interest in practitioner research and the use of research in education.

Contact details

c.sharp@nfer.ac.uk

4 Searching for literature

You've decided what it is you want to research, defined your question and planned out your project. How do you set this in a context that makes it sensible to others? How do you show that what you're trying to do is worthwhile and that your results are worth finding? **Alison Lawson** and **Pauline Benefield** explain the benefits of a literature search and how to go about doing it.

You need to be confident that you have found as much of the available evidence as possible by searching the literature on your chosen topic in a systematic way. Your search must be open to scrutiny so it can be replicated and updated. A less than comprehensive search can lead to the risk of missing potentially important studies and thus presenting a distorted view of findings.

Why do it?

Setting your own research in the context of other literature on the same or similar subject adds credibility to your work. It broadens your awareness of other research in the area and provides background information and data that corroborates what you've found. It also ensures that you are not duplicating research that has already been done by someone else. Searching the literature may also challenge your

assumptions – you may find that the literature contradicts commonly held points of view or says exactly the opposite to what you were hoping to find. Sometimes, researchers decide to revise their original line of enquiry to take account of new information that has been found during the literature search.

How to do it

The first stage is to define your key research questions very clearly, because these can be used to plan your decisions about searches, inclusion criteria and themes for your research. You then need to identify the relevant sources that will be used for your search and if possible enlist the help of a librarian or information expert.

It may be helpful first of all to look at a bibliography or previous review to get a feel for the literature, and also to search databases of current research to find out whether any research is already being carried out on your chosen topic.

There are several ways of identifying the potential sources of literature, such as:

- hand searches

- keyword searches in electronic journal (and other) databases

- searching the internet and library catalogues

- using sources recommended by personal and professional contacts within your field of study

- using sources you're already familiar with, e.g. course texts.

Identifying key journals in your field and hand searching their contents, either in hard copy or electronically via publishers' websites, can be an important strategy in finding material. All journals and articles are not automatically included in electronic databases, and even then you are dependent on studies being indexed correctly.

Electronic databases focus on a particular topic or discipline, and it is always a good idea to search as many of these sources as possible, depending on time and resources available. Social science databases are varied in terms of both quality and coverage and many are subscription based.

Electronic sources alone will fail to locate all the relevant information as a lot of literature is not available

Case study 4.1

I spent months researching my chosen subject, and immersed myself in the literature, which I really enjoyed. However, after a while, I realised that literature from 2003 was saying the same as the literature from 1954, and that the thinking hadn't really moved on. I began to think that my research was only going to say the same thing again, and that it would be no use to anyone, even though I found it interesting. So I scrapped the project and embarked on a new one. It was a tough decision, but I wanted my research to be interesting and useful to other people, too.
Research student

through normal publishing channels. This includes reports published independently by organisations, working papers, conference papers and publications with short print runs. This is often referred to as grey literature.

Methods of identifying this include internet searches of pertinent websites and subject gateways. Material on the latter is selected, classified and evaluated by networks of subject specialists. Many library catalogues are now available online and can also be useful sources.

Contact with experts in your chosen field is another recommended method of finding material as they can often help identify work that has yet to be published. This can be done either personally or through an email discussion list. Contact with others working in the same field may lead to literature that you have not uncovered in other ways.

This chapter will consider searching in electronic databases in particular, as these are often the main starting point for literature searches.

Search parameters

Once you have identified your sources you also need to decide on your search parameters, such as timescale, geographical scope, age range and types of literature.

What is the timescale of your research?

You need to establish the beginning and end dates for your research and on what criteria this is based. An example would be literature published after an important piece of legislation was introduced or to continue the work of an earlier review in the area. Setting an end date is also helpful, because it means you do not have to update the review as new pieces of work are published.

What is the geographical scope of your review?

This is quite often only the UK but may include other English-speaking countries. Limiting your review to studies written in English is a recognised source of bias, so this must be clearly stated in your search strategy.

What is the age range or educational level of your study population?

If your research is limited to one educational level, this will help to narrow down the search results.

> **Case study 4.2**
>
> I was doing some research about ICT and found thousands of results on my keyword searches in a journal database. Then I thought that anything about ICT that was more than five or six years old would be more of historical interest than practical use in my research, so I narrowed the search down to articles published after 1 January 2000. Bingo! My search results were reduced to only 150 potentially useful articles.
>
> Teacher researcher

What types of literature will your review cover?

Do you want to include published studies only (these are easiest to find on databases) or do you want to include unpublished theses, newspaper articles, opinion pieces, grey literature and current research? Including different types of literature in the review will give different viewpoints, but excluding them will narrow your search and make it more pointed.

When limiting your search in any way, you must be aware of the possibility of introducing a bias to the results. For example, if you limit your results to articles in English, you may miss a ground-breaking study that was published in Swedish. It is important, therefore, to recognise any potential bias in the results by keeping a record of the limits you set on your search and then reporting these when you come to write up your results.

Starting your search in an electronic database

Think about your research question and break it down into its component parts, mapping out all the different subject elements. Compile a list of words and phrases that describe these different elements and that you can use as keywords in your search. Collect as many potential search terms as possible at this stage by thinking of synonyms and listing American as well as British terms, depending on the

> **Box 4.1 Listing keywords to use in your search**
>
> Research question: Is boys' behaviour related to attainment at key stage 2?
>
> Possible keywords and phrases:
> - behaviour
> - pupil behaviour
> - behavior
> - pupil behavior
> - attainment
> - academic achievement
> - boys
> - males
> - sex differences
> - key stage 2
> - KS2
> - primary education
> - boys' behaviour
> - boys' behavior
> - boys' attainment
> - boys' academic achievement

databases to be searched. Once you have identified a few highly relevant articles, you can use their keywords to supplement your list.

The aim is to identify all material which deals specifically with your research question and to exclude any which is irrelevant. It is very easy to become sidetracked and waste a lot of time following up items of marginal interest. See Box 4.1 for an example of listing and combining keywords for a specific research question.

Plan which keywords to use for each database and then start your search. The larger databases have controlled vocabularies or thesauri, and searching using these subject headings will retrieve the information most relevant to your chosen topic. To ensure your search is comprehensive, or to search for a concept which is not adequately covered by the subject terms, it is also necessary to search free text. This means searching for specific terms or phrases within other parts of the document, such as the title and abstract. If the database you're using does not have a controlled vocabulary of keywords, then you'll have to search free text and be careful which keywords you use.

To combine the different concepts in your search in a logical way you will need to use 'Boolean operators', which allow you to broaden or restrict a search. The main operators are 'OR' and 'AND', the former allowing the broadening of your search by a combination of concepts and the latter restricting it by combining them with each other. For example:

Box 4.2 Combining keywords and phrases in your search

Research question: Is boys' behaviour related to attainment at key stage 2?

Possible combinations of keywords and phrases:

- boys AND behaviour
- boys AND behaviour
- boys AND attainment
- boys AND key stage 2
- behaviour AND attainment
- behavior AND attainment
- behaviour AND key stage 2
- behavior AND key stage 2
- attainment AND key stage 2
- boys AND behaviour AND attainment
- boys AND behavior AND attainment

- boys AND key stage 2 AND behaviour
- boys AND key stage 2 AND behavior
- boys AND key stage 2 AND attainment
- behaviour AND attainment AND boys AND key stage 2

Once you have done these searches, you can combine the results, for example:

- boys OR sex differences) AND (behaviour OR behaviour OR pupil behaviou) AND (attainment OR academic achievement) AND (key stage 2 OR KS2 OR primary education).

This will retrieve all the records addressing your keywords.

- 'achievement' OR 'curriculum' will give you all articles that contain either 'achievement' or 'curriculum', which will broaden your search

- 'achievement' AND 'curriculum' will give you all articles that contain both 'achievement' and 'curriculum', thereby narrowing your search.

See Box 4.2 for an example of combining keywords and phrases The vast majority of databases also have the truncation facility, which picks up variants of a term, for example, searching for 'organi*' will pick up:

- organise
- organize
- organised
- organized
- organisation
- organization
- organisational
- organizational
- organisationally
- organizationally
- organising
- organizing
- organic
- organically
- organist
- organism

Most databases have help screens that will help you to familiarise yourself with these commands and how to use them.

Other related searches

If you find highly relevant documents in your search, it is useful to scan the reference listed at the end of these – often you can identify further studies that may not have emerged from the original searches because the keywords are slightly different.

You may find that key authors in the field turn up often in searches or in references lists, so it may be a good idea to search for them individually, too.

key authors in the field turn up often

Keeping a record of your results

The larger databases have a variety of options for saving and transmitting search results, which may be very useful. Make sure that you can keep track of what you've found – keep your own record of searches completed and literature found.

The search terms and combinations of terms that have been used for each individual database should be documented and made explicit. This will be useful if you want to replicate a search you have completed in one database in another. This will also be important when you write up your results, as you will be able to show the systematic and thorough nature of your search.

What next?

While finding the literature can be rewarding, it can be daunting to face reading all the material and sorting through it. In the next chapter we'll look at how to:

- make useful notes as you go along
- limit and focus your results to match your research question
- take stock at the end of the exercise to see what 'shape' the information is
- use the results of your search to set your own work in context.

Further reading

Brettle, A. and Grant, M.J. (2004). *Finding the Evidence for Practice: a Workbook for Health Professionals.* London: Churchill Livingstone.

Evidence Network (2006). *Searching Guidelines* [online]. Available: http://evidencenetwork.org/Searching.html [9 March 2007].

Fink, A. (1998). *Conducting Research Literature Reviews: from Paper to the Internet.* London: Sage.

Gash, S. (2000). *Effective Literature Searching for Research.* Second edn. Aldershot: Gower.

Gomersall, A. (2005). 'Finding the evidence: looking further afield', *Evidence & Policy*, 1, 2, 269–85.

Hart, C. (2001). *Doing a Literature Search: a Comprehensive Guide for the Social Sciences.* London: Sage.

Petticrew, M. and Roberts, H. (2006). *Systematic Reviews in the Social Sciences: a Practical Guide.* Oxford: Blackwell.

Weblinks

CERUK Plus
www.ceruk.ac.uk/ceruk
British Library
www.bl.uk
British Education Internet Resource Catalogue
brs.leeds.ac.uk/%7Ebeiwww/beirc.htm
Education Resources Information Center
www.eric.ed.gov

Social Care Online
www.scie-socialcareonline.org.uk
EPPI-Centre
eppi.ioe.ac.uk/cms
UK Educational Evidence Portal
www.eep.ac.uk/Main/Default.aspx

About the authors

Alison Lawson was an HE lecturer for two years, tutoring HND, degree and postgraduate students on research methods for dissertations and projects. Her own research has used mainly qualitative methods and is in the areas of vocational education, organisational studies, business and management. She is Marketing and Publishing Manager at the NFER.

Pauline Benefield is Deputy Librarian at NFER and has worked on reviews for a wide range of clients, including TDA, DfES and QCA. She has experience of using systematic procedures in searching a wide range of sources, including electronic and print sources and grey literature, in order to identify all the available research evidence, as well as in ensuring the quality assurance of all bibliographic citations.

Contact details

Alison Lawson
a.lawson@nfer.ac.uk

5 What to do with the results of your literature search

Chapter 4 explored how to go about conducting a literature search. In this follow-up chapter **Alison Lawson** tackles the issue of what to do next.

Embarking on research can be exciting. Doing all the searches can take time and be gruelling, but there is definitely an excitement that builds as you find articles about your chosen topic. In an effort to be exhaustive within your set search parameters, you've conducted your search and you've got lots of abstracts or full articles as a result. Sometimes, all you have is a citation and you'll have to look a bit harder just to find the abstract. The problem is, how do you tackle what might be hundreds of abstracts and articles when time is limited? Wading through them all will not only use up your time, but wear you out and possibly make you tire of the research project. But fear not – there are solutions!

Dealing with abstracts

The quickest way to cut down what you have to read is to read the abstracts of the articles you have found, rather than the whole article. The abstract should give you a good idea or whether it is worth your while reading the whole article. Sometimes, the title of an article can sound as if it's exactly what you want, but the abstract makes it clear that it isn't suitable after all. For example, an article entitled 'Perceptions of the impact of workforce remodelling' might sound perfect for your research until you read the abstract and find out it's about workforce remodelling in the NHS, rather than in education. Reading the abstracts and discarding those that aren't appropriate or relevant to your research question will reduce the number of articles on your desk for reading.

However, sometimes abstracts aren't very good. If you find the abstract isn't very helpful, try reading the introduction, key findings and conclusion instead – these sections should give you enough information for you to decide whether it is worth your while reading the whole article.

Reading articles

Even when you have discarded those articles that are not suitable, you will still have a large number of articles to read, and it will be useful to have a strategy for reading these in a systematic way, so that you get as much as possible from each one and don't forget what you've read. Here are two ideas that might help.

First, sort your articles into categories, so that the mass of articles becomes several more digestible bundles. For example, you could have one bundle related to each strand of your research or to each research question. Other ways of sorting the articles are to rate their importance or relevance on a short scale, where 1 is very important/relevant, 2 is quite important and informative, and 3 is not as important/relevant, but with some very interesting information that might be useful. Articles may also be organised by their age or by their date of publication relative to a particular initiative or intervention. If you use more than one of these ways to sort your articles, you can achieve some very pointed categories, e.g. articles related to each research strand, rated by importance/relevance and published within the last year.

Second, make notes as you go along. This sounds obvious, but it's not necessarily easy. When you come to refer back to your notes, you need to be able to understand them and marshal them into an argument. It

> **Case study 5.1**
>
> I found a really useful article – exactly on my subject and saying really interesting things, even with a couple of case studies. I was so excited that I explained it all, in immense detail to my boyfriend over dinner. While his expression gradually glazed over and he said, 'That sounds great, sweetheart' I found that I'd crystallised exactly what I wanted to say about that article and how it fitted in with my argument, so I had to write it down before I forgot. My boyfriend was very patient...

might help to create a table with set headings so you know what to look for in each article, like the one shown in Table 5.1. If you spend some time before you read the articles setting up the table you'll use to note down information from them, this will save you a lot of time later. Create the table to be as easy as possible for you to use as you're reading and when you come to look at your notes in the future. Ideally, you want your table of notes to be so systematic and informative that you won't need to re-read the original articles in full for information when you write up the results of your search. It's a good idea to make a note of any particularly pertinent quotations or extracts and the pages they're on, in case you want to use them later.

Taking stock of the information

When taking stock of the information you've gathered, always think back to the research question(s). It's very easy to get distracted by interesting articles that aren't really relevant to your research, but have fired your enthusiasm.

Your reading of articles and your note taking will help you to get a feel for the 'shape' of your information. You may have started off looking for one thing and found that the literature is much more concentrated on something else. You may find that you're able to group the articles into

two or three groups that fit well together – this will help when you come to discuss and analyse what you have found. You may find it useful to talk about what you've read and about what you've found. If you have a research supervisor or tutor, this is where they come in. If you don't, then speaking to other researchers or other practitioners interested in research can be very useful. Sometimes, saying things out load helps you to understand what you've learned.

Be brave

You will probably read a large number of articles. Don't feel that you have to read *everything*. For a small-scale study you may not need more than half a dozen key texts. If you find that much

Table 5.1 An example of how to organise note taking when reading your articles

Citation	Relevant to research question ...	Key findings	Design and methods used	Sample used	Star rating	Comments
Author, date, article title, journal name, volume and pages	Relate to your own research	As relevant to your research	What kind of research was it? How was it done? How many parts were there to the project?	Who was involved? How many? Any other important characteristics?	For example: 1 – interesting for back-ground 2 – makes good points 3 – especially relevant to hypothesis	Anything else you want to add for quick reference later

of the literature says pretty much the same thing, then you only need to use a few of the sources – pick the best ones and leave the others. If you're short of time, discard the articles that are interesting, but not really relevant – for example, some might fall outside your search parameters by being from the wrong country or too old. You can always read these at a later date when you're not under pressure to get your research finished.

You may also find that you have to discard articles because they are not of a high-enough quality. For example, if the way the research was designed means that the results aren't valid or replicable in other settings, or if the conclusions don't actually answer the research questions, or if you're unsure that the methods used were sufficiently rigorous. Don't be afraid to set high standards.

It can be difficult to decide which sources to discard and which to keep, especially as it may have taken you a long time to search for the literature, read it and take notes. But it's important to remember that you don't have to include everything just because it's relevant – a few well-chosen, key texts are more useful than a scattering of many texts. You might find it useful to use a tool like the one shown in Figure 5.1 for deciding what to keep and what to discard. Plot your articles on the axes and include those that are important AND relevant to your study, then those that are relevant only, then those that are important only. Articles that, on reflection, are neither all that important and not particularly relevant should be discarded.

If you decide to keep a lot of articles, you might achieve breadth but only superficial coverage. When reducing the number of articles in order to achieve more depth of discussion, you are likely to have less breadth. This should make your work more focussed.

Figure 5.1 Deciding which articles to include in your study

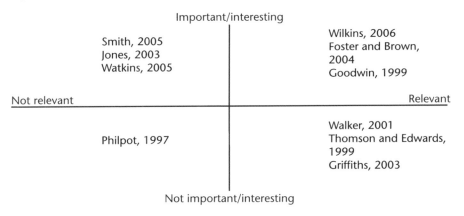

Case study 5.2

I'd planned to use about 1500 words to write up the literature and I'd got 15 articles. If I allowed 100 words for introduction, 300 for drawing all the themes together and another 100 for summing up at the end, that only left me with 1000 words – 67 words per article. It just wasn't enough! So I was brutal, and cut the articles down to only ten. This made the write-up more in-depth and meant I had more scope to analyse what I'd found, although it was tough to leave aside articles I'd enjoyed very much and were pertinent to my argument. I had to face the fact that I didn't have to include everything, just because it was relevant.

Writing up the results

Writing up the results will be covered in a future article in the *Tool-kit* series in the journal, *practical research for education*, but here are some tips about what to think about.

- Group your results under appropriate headings, perhaps relating to the themes of your research, or to themes that became clear as you went through the literature.

- Always think back to the research question and make sure that what you're saying is relevant.

- Be critical of what you read – analyse and synthesise what you find, rather than simply describing what you find.

- Use the results of your search to set your own work in context.

Further reading

Boaz, A., Ashby, D. and Young, K. (2002). *Systematic Reviews: What Have They Got to Offer Evidence Based Policy and Practice?* (Working Paper 2). London: ESRC, UK Centre for Evidence Based Policy and Practice.

Wallace, M. and Poulson, L. (2003). 'Critical reading for self-critical writing.' In: Wallace, M. and Poulson, L. (Eds) *Learning to Read Critically in Educational Leadership and Management*. London: Sage.

Weblinks

Most university websites have information for students about how to conduct literature reviews, and many of these are accessible to the general public, too.

Wikipedia has some useful general information about literature reviews. **http://en.wikipedia.org/wiki/Literature_review**

Information about systematic reviews for evaluating policy is available at the Policy Hub.
www.policyhub.gov.uk/evaluating_policy/magenta_book/chapter2.asp

About the author

Alison Lawson is Marketing and Publishing Manager at NFER. In 2006, she completed her PhD about information and communications technology and organisational change. Alison would like to thank her colleague, Pauline Benefield, Deputy Librarian at NFER and trainer in systematic reviews, for her advice and comments on this chapter.

Contact details

Alison Lawson
a.lawson@nfer.ac.uk

6 Collecting evidence of pupil work

Real-life evidence from pupils can add richness, depth and a new perspective to a research project. **Helen Betts** and **Bethan Burge** outline some of the issues to consider when planning to collect evidence of pupils' work as part of a research project.

This chapter is about the process of collecting evidence of pupil performance. It provides:

- an overview of the value of collecting evidence of pupil work as part of the research process
- guidance on how to collect evidence effectively
- the different types of evidence you might collect, including written work, a creative piece or a snippet of conversation
- case-study examples.

Who is this chapter for?

This chapter gives useful information for those conducting their own research in an educational context. For example:

- students completing courses in education
- researchers within universities and other organisations.

In addition to these groups, much of this information and advice may by useful to teachers conducting action research in their own classrooms.

Why include evidence of pupil performance in research?

During the course of a research project, it is sometimes necessary to find out about how pupils work in a real classroom situation. You may wish to add to your understanding of an educational issue, and find out how theories relate to real classroom practice. You may have begun the research process with a literature search (see chapter 4) and have your own observations too, but gathering first-hand evidence to back up the literature helps to triangulate the evidence. It also provides real-life case-study information from up-to-date contexts. Whatever the reason, there is no doubt that real examples of pupils' work or classroom discussions add a richness and authenticity to your research. The examples of research projects given in Box 6.1 vary in terms of focus and research question, but an integral aspect of each is the need to gather evidence about pupils' performance and/or response.

Collecting pupil evidence effectively

Teachers – researchers in their own classrooms

Although many of the points and pieces of advice in this chapter apply to larger scale research projects, they apply equally well to small pieces of research, including those conducted by teachers in their own classrooms.

Issues to consider

Involve children in your research as much as possible. This means not just collecting evidence of their work, but explaining to them why you are interested in this particular aspect of their work and how they are helping you.

If you want to collect evidence of a presentation, class discussion or piece of artwork, make sure you have the necessary resources available in school to allow you to make a record of these activities.

If you are planning to share the outcomes of your research, you need to obtain parental permission for photographs or video footage, and if

> **Box 6.1 Examples of research projects**
>
> A student completing an education degree wants to find out how the principles of feedback in assessment for learning can help pupils to improve their presentation skills. A university researcher wants to trial a task with pupils to evaluate its accessibility for key stage 3 pupils with special educational needs. A researcher wants to compare the performance of pupils working at different national curriculum levels in art and design. A student completing a masters degree in education wants to find out whether girls are more creative in their writing than boys. A teacher doing research in their own classroom might be introducing a new scheme of work or monitoring the progress of a particular group of children.

you want to identify individuals by name.

Your research may benefit from the involvement of other colleagues in your school. If you have a teaching assistant available, you might want to use their time to help you collect evidence from a wider group of pupils. If you wish to involve other class teachers, it may simply be a case of talking about your project during a staff meeting in order to explain the aims of the research and answer any questions.

If you are doing research in your own school, access should not be problematic, but the issues raised elsewhere in this chapter are important if you hope to involve other colleagues or schools in your research.

Researchers not in schools – getting schools on board

Once you have clearly established the focus and aims of your research (for more information on planning your research project see chapter 1), the first step in collecting evidence of pupil outcomes is contacting schools to ask them to be involved in your research project. For smaller scale projects this may mean inviting local schools to take part. It will be necessary to gain the headteacher's permission before using a school – an initial letter outlining the project is a good starting point. Where your project requires a great deal of teacher input, it can often be advantageous to target schools with whom you have had previous contact, who are perhaps more likely to invest time in

helping with your research. In the case of projects that require a larger amount of pupil evidence, it may be necessary to draw a representative sample of schools (for more information on drawing a school/pupil sample see chapter 2).

Whatever the scope of your research project, it is important that the headteachers and teachers you approach are aware of the potential time commitment involved in gathering this kind of evidence. The reason for this is that collecting evidence of pupil outcomes can place more of a burden on schools and teachers than questionnaire surveys. For example, you may be asking the

how pupils work in a real classroom situation

class teacher to substitute a lesson they had already spent time planning with the activity you would like pupils to engage with. You will also need to make every effort to work around the school timetable. After investing time in your project, teachers may be interested to know the outcomes of your research – feedback to schools is something worth considering at an early stage.

Planning your evidence collection

If you are working on a smaller scale research project, visiting all the schools involved in order to collect all the evidence yourself might be possible. However, for larger scale research projects it may not be feasible for you to gather all the evidence. Visiting large numbers of schools can be very resource intensive, particularly if the schools you have selected cover a wide geographical area. It may therefore be necessary to involve teachers in the process of evidence collection. Both collecting evidence in person and involving teachers have advantages and disadvantages. These approaches are explored further below.

Collecting the evidence yourself: making the most of your visits

If you do plan to visit schools yourself, you need to make sure that prior to your visit, the teacher involved fully understands both your role and theirs in this aspect of the research. You may

plan to present some materials to pupils and initiate a discussion to gauge their reactions, or your research project may require you to take much more of an observational role in the classroom. In both cases, it is important teachers understand what is required of them, and that they are made aware of the aims of your research. In explaining this purpose, you should also emphasise to teachers that your role is not to monitor or evaluate their teaching; it is crucial they understand that your focus is pupil performance. This should be made clear from the outset.

In order that the evidence you collect contributes meaningfully to your research, it is crucial that the teachers involved understand the purpose of the project. For example, if the focus of the research is individual pupil ability then it is important that the pupils work on their own rather than in small groups. For this reason it is helpful to speak to the class teachers directly before they begin to collect evidence, so that they have some appreciation of why you need to collect evidence and how it might be used, analysed or reported. It might also be useful to give them a written summary of your research aims. Provide the teacher with as much information as you can, without overloading them with unnecessary details. Make sure it is clear whether the results of your research will be kept confidential or be made public and available to others. Box 6.2 shows some of the questions you might need to answer when

Box 6.2 Briefing teachers: what they will want to know

- What are you trying to find out or show?
- How much time do I need to commit?
- What exactly do I have to do?
- What will my pupils have to do?
- Is the evidence collected confidential?
- What information will be collected?
- What will you do with the results? Will I receive any feedback about my pupils?
- Is this the only involvement I/my class/my school will have in the project?

Box 6.3 Ensuring confidentiality within your research

When you brief both teachers and pupils, you should make it clear to them that their responses are confidential and that they will not be identified in any of the research findings. This may be particularly important for headteachers, who may not wish to take part in the research if their schools can be identified in any research reports.

Remember!

If you do collect evidence in the form of photographs or video footage showing images of pupils, you must obtain parental permission in advance. If it is anticipated that these images will be published and therefore in the public domain, you must get additional permission from parents to do so.

briefing teachers and Box 6.3 gives more information about confidentiality issues.

Although for some research projects you might want a random sample of pupils, in other cases you may want the teacher to select pupils that meet criteria that are important for your research aims. Therefore, teacher involvement can be particularly important when selecting which pupils you will work with during your visit. Before your visit you may wish to ask teachers to identify suitable pupils. Box 6.4 provides an example of when this

kind of teacher input has been particularly valuable.

It is important to remember that the way you select pupils will have an impact on the extent to which you can generalise your findings.

It may also be desirable, or necessary, to talk to the pupils involved in your research, perhaps providing them with a short

Box 6.4 Trialling reading tasks for lower-ability pupils

For this project, the researcher wanted to gauge the suitability of reading task materials developed for children working below expected National Curriculum levels.

Both special schools and mainstream schools were visited to collect evidence of pupil performance on the tasks. In the mainstream schools, teacher involvement was vital in ensuring that the researcher worked with pupils who were at the right level and represented a wide range of reading difficulties.

introduction about the purposes of your visit. This could help increase pupil motivation and engagement, and will help you get the most out of your research visits.

Asking teachers to collect evidence: making the most of their expertise and involvement

Asking teachers to collect examples of their own pupils' performance can be a valuable approach when collecting evidence of this kind. It means that the pupil work is produced in a more natural classroom environment, and therefore may be more representative of the work the pupil would ordinarily do. Making use of teachers' expertise in

this way can be of particular importance if the project requires you to collect evidence of individual/group presentations or class discussions; less confident pupils may feel nervous about or be reluctant to take part in this kind of oral activity in front of researchers they have only met briefly before beginning the activity.

You may ask a teacher to collect evidence of pupil work from a whole class, or to sample pupils randomly, for example, by selecting every sixth pupil from the class register. Alternatively, you may wish to focus on specific groups of pupils, for example, all those working within a particular level, those who are learning English as an additional language or those who have been identified as gifted and talented. In these instances, the class teacher is best placed to select the pupils in order to best fulfil the aims of your research.

Collecting different types of evidence

Some kinds of evidence are easier to collect than others. A written piece of work can simply be collected or copied. A piece of creative work such as an object made in a design and technology class can be photographed. However, some non-written evidence is ephemeral – it may be a snippet of conversation between pupils working in groups or pairs, a contribution to an oral presentation, or a comment to or by a teacher. This is often the case when what you are interested in is a pupil's thought processes, reasoning or decision-making ability.

This is the hardest kind of evidence to collect, particularly if you are relying on someone else to capture it for you (for example, a teacher working with a class of 30 lively pupils). Although the ideal solution might be to focus on an individual/small group for a whole lesson, this is not always possible in practice and an animated discussion can be difficult to document accurately!

In order to make a record of all these kinds of pupil outcomes, you might want to consider using audio or visual recording equipment during your visits to schools. This can help you during the analysis or reporting phase of your project, as you can revisit the rich evidence you have collected. If, as described in the previous section, a teacher is collecting evidence on your behalf, you also need to ensure that they have the equipment they need in order to assist with the research. For example, if you have asked them to record a group discussion or presentation, it may be necessary to supply audio-visual equipment. It is also worth spending some time ensuring they are relatively confident using this equipment. To make sure that any audio or visual evidence collected by teachers is not wasted, it might be necessary to advise carrying this out in a quiet area of the school or classroom. This will ensure that the evidence is of sufficient

quality to be of use in the research, and applies equally whether it is you or a teacher collecting the evidence. Again, when collecting any evidence in which teachers or students may be identifiable, ensure you have the correct permission to do so.

So why not have a go yourself?

Here are the key questions to ask yourself at various points during the process of collecting evidence of pupil performance.

Before you begin

- How will this kind of evidence enrich my research?

- What type of evidence will best suit the aims of my research, and what is the most efficient way of obtaining it?

- Which groups of pupils would I like to involve in the project?

- How will I present the evidence I collect?

Getting started

- Am I able to collect the evidence myself, or should I involve teachers directly?

- How many schools do I need to involve?

- How will I go about encouraging teachers and their pupils to take part in my research?

Carrying out the research

- How will I explain my aims to those involved?
- What can I do to make sure the quality of my evidence is high?
- How can I ensure confidentiality?
- How will I feed back to schools?

A final word

So what do you do with all the evidence you have collected? The great thing about this kind of data is that it is extremely rich and authentic. If you want to make the most of the evidence you have, it is important to allow plenty of time to study and analyse what you have collected. This will enable you to identify key points of interest, and to select the pieces of work that best exemplify your findings.

Weblinks

These weblinks provide an introduction to some of the work NFER has been involved in using this kind of qualitative research method.

Assessment for learning
http://www.nfer.ac.uk/publications /pdfs/downloadable/AssessmentforL earning.pdf

Support for teacher assessment in teaching English in Wales
http://www.nfer.ac.uk/research-areas/pims-data/summaries/key-stag e-2-english-in-wales-teacher.cfm
Curriculum in action
http://curriculum.qca.org.uk/curric ulum-in-action/index.aspx

About the authors

Helen Betts trained as a primary teacher before joining the NFER in 2003, where she is a senior research officer. Helen has been involved in the development of a range of classroom assessment materials.

Bethan Burge is a senior research officer at NFER, and has been involved in the development of a range of classroom materials for teachers. In addition to her test-development work Bethan has been involved in other assessment research and evaluations.

Contact details

Bethan Burge
b.burge@nfer.ac.uk

Afterword: action research in a learning school

Sharon Butler, Assistant Head CPD and School Development,
Newstead Wood School

First, a bit of history. Teacher-led research has been a feature of Newstead Wood School's School Development Plans since 2000, funded initially by internal project awards, then external grants (such as the Independent State School Partnership grant), and affiliation with interested organisations, whether the Specialist Schools and Academies Trust, National Academy for Gifted and Talented Youth, Department for Children, Schools and Families or London Challenge.

Elizabeth Allen, our headteacher, certainly wanted research outcomes, but her main aim was a shift in school culture, a staff questioning ideas and methods, and thinking as tutors and teachers about the nature of learning itself. And she wanted to see that thinking in curriculum design, assessment and lessons.

The big question was and still is: how do students learn? And how do we create the best climate for the best learning? Questions about learning pose themselves just as urgently in every school, no matter what kind of school you happen to be.

Becoming research-engaged has been exciting and beneficial. It has raised our awareness of barriers to learning, built teaching repertoire and expertise (especially, in our case, with gifted and talented students) and involved us in wider educational development and debate. It has inspired our students to greater independent learning through their ongoing involvement in research and the related activities of student leadership.

Because virtually all our students are 'gifted and talented', we investigate the impact of self-esteem on learning, raising achievement through consultation, and the effect of interactive rather than didactic teaching. Our research partnerships have led us via assessment for learning to student voice. We are redesigning our curriculum, most immediately for thematic education in year 7.

Today, Newstead remains at the forefront of national league tables. Our engineering specialism focuses on creativity, problem solving and thinking skills, with languages our second specialism. We are a Deep Leadership Hub for the Specialist Schools and Academies Trust, working in Student Leadership. Our School Development Plan knits together Deep Leadership, Learning and Support. Our Head Girls Team attends the Asia-Pacific Young Leaders Summit in Singapore and presents nationally on their experience of school leadership, helping students find solutions to real problems, including organising their own funding. Underpinning this, an eco-team of five leads our Sustainable Schools Programme. Elizabeth Allen has just been appointed a National Leader in Education.

And what of the future? Newstead's developments now have a research phase when the learning process is co-constructed by students, parents and staff. Individual teachers step forward to pilot initiatives as research projects within the School Development Plan, reporting on the outcomes within their performance management review in a variety of forums. NFER's *Tool-kits* provide valuable encouragement and guidance for the whole school community. Those big questions about learning can never be finally answered, but school-based research is key to doing the best for every child.

July 2008